# Stephen

## *The Fascinating Story Of A Basketball Superstar – Stephen Curry – Best Shooter In Basketball History*

By Steve Peyton

© Copyright 2016 by Steve Peyton Publishing - All rights reserved.

This document is geared towards providing exact and reliable information in regards to the topic and issue covered. The publication is sold with the idea that the publisher is not required to render accounting, officially permitted, or otherwise, qualified services. If advice is necessary, legal or professional, a practiced individual in the profession should be ordered.

- From a Declaration of Principles which was accepted and approved equally by a Committee of the American Bar Association and a Committee of Publishers and Associations.

In no way is it legal to reproduce, duplicate, or transmit any part of this document in either electronic means or in printed format. Recording of this publication is strictly prohibited and any storage of this document is not allowed unless with written permission from the publisher. All rights reserved.

The information provided herein is stated to be truthful and consistent, in that any liability, in terms of inattention or otherwise, by any usage or abuse of any policies, processes, or directions contained within is the solitary and utter responsibility of the recipient reader. Under no circumstances will any legal responsibility or blame be held against the publisher for any reparation, damages, or monetary loss due to the information herein, either directly or indirectly.

Respective authors own all copyrights not held by the

publisher.

The information herein is offered for informational purposes solely, and is universal as so. The presentation of the information is without contract or any type of guarantee assurance.

The trademarks that are used are without any consent, and the publication of the trademark is without permission or backing by the trademark owner. All trademarks and brands within this book are for clarifying purposes only and are the owned by the owners themselves, not affiliated with this document.

# Table of Contents

# Introduction

I want to thank you and congratulate you for taking the time to read, *"Stephen Curry: The Fascinating Story Of A Basketball Superstar – Stephen Curry – Best Shooter In Basketball History"*

This book will give you the fascinating story of the basketball superstar, Stephen Curry.

If you do a search on the internet, you will find slideshows of the house that Stephen Curry grew up in. The house, built by his parents in 1996 when Curry turned eight, stands on a sixteen-acre plot on the outskirts of Charlotte city center, North Carolina. It is a big house, 6 bedroomed house.

It is here, that everything began. Curry's father, Dell, played for the Hornets, the local NBA franchise as a shooting guard, and had won the 6th man of the year award in the league. One cannot help but wonder if Stephen inherited the shooting touch from his father.

The league's enthusiasts have had the pleasure of watching some of the best shooters the game has ever seen in action, including the likes of Larry Bird, Pete Maravich, Reggie Miller, and Ray Allen. However, most of these enthusiasts believe that Stephen Curry may very well be the greatest shooter in the history of basketball. While this is still debatable, his performances have repeatedly proven that this statement might actually hold some truth, especially to loyal Allen or Miller fans.

On February 27, 2013, Steph, one of Curry's fond nicknames, brought Madison Square garden to life with a career best achievement of 54 points, including eleven of thirteen from deep. He is also the league's record holder for 3 pointers made in one season – 272, which he set in the 2012 to 2013 season, taking over from Allen.

Despite his immense achievements, which he accumulated over many years of hard work, life was not a smooth road for Steph; because your father is an ex-NBA player does not mean you are going to become one as well. For instance, Michael Jordan's son, Marcus Jordan, is yet to play a game in the NBA.

Even though Curry had a great reputation as a son of a retired NBA player, he was not exactly a popular choice in high school basketball. Because of his small stature, the high school coaches often dismissed him, and most of the other players did not believe he had what it took to be successful at college basketball.

Fortunately, he did not allow this setback to hold him from realizing his dream; he continued playing and went on to thrive at the game playing for a small college, simply known as Davidson, located in Charlotte, close to their home.

In 2008, during the NCAA Tournament, basketball fans watched as a repeat of the biblical David vs. Goliath match took place, with Curry singlehandedly taking down, one by one, the "gigantic" college Teams until his team ran out of 'steam' in a game against Kansas in the Elite 8. Since he was at the center of Davidson's wins, this run pushed Steph to the spotlight.

Through the Golden State Warriors, he got included in the

2009 NBA draft, but because of stubborn ankle injuries in the first 3 years, basketball fans started comparing him to Grant Hill whom because of constant injuries early in his career was never able to achieve his full potential.

Despite his injuries, and the comparison to Grant Hill, Steph proved the critics wrong, bounced back, and proved to be in excellent health; he then went on to set record after record on his way to stardom during the last 2 seasons.

Curry has brought relevance to the once latent Golden State franchise. With another lethal shooter, Klay Thompson by his side, and a steep roster led by the likes of Andre Iguodala, Harrison Barnes, Andrew Bogut, and David Lee, the Warriors are set to make another deep run at this season's playoffs.

Great men, men who deserve emulation, are those that size what seem like insurmountable odds, and then do everything in their power to triumph over these odds. Coming from a humble, albeit advantaged background because of his dad's basketball experience, where everyone thought he would amount to nothing in playing basketball, Curry has proven that, indeed, what people think does not have to influence what you become. As the rest of this UNAUTHORIZED Stephen Curry Biography will show, from a disadvantaged background, a herculean legend can rise.

Thanks again for downloading this book, I hope you enjoy it!

# Section 1: Early Childhood

Since his father was an ex-NBA shooting guard, Stephen had the optimal platform to learn and mature into the striking sharpshooter he became. Stephen's love for basketball developed at an early age. According to Dell Curry, his father, Steph's first basketball game happened when he was just 2 weeks old. Although he has grown into his own man, it is obvious that Curry learned a lot about the game by watching his father in action.

Wardell Stephen Curry II was born in Akron, Ohio, on 14 March 1988. He had a superbly sporty background back in Ohio, with two professional athletes, his parents, Dell and Sonya Curry by his side. Dell Curry, his father, is a retired NBA shooting guard, once famous for his excellent shooting. While he played for 5 different teams in 16 seasons, his most famous stint was between 1988 and 1998, where his star shone the brightest as he played for the Charlotte Hornets. In his glory day, it was a usual occurrence to see a young Stephen watching his father's games from the courtside.

Steph's mother, Sonya, on the other hand, was a celebrated volleyball player. She and Dell were both college stars who met at Virginia Tech. Sonya was a basketball fanatic, and it was not long before she caught Dell's attention. They fell in love, and as they say, the rest is history.

When Curry was in the 1st grade, Sonya begun a Christian school in Montessori, and this greatly contributed to cementing the family bond and bringing them together. For the years following this, the Curry siblings were accompanied to school by their aunt, mom, and grandmother. It is in this school that Steph learned about accountability and independence.

Steph's mother, Sonya, was a very stern disciplinarian. She recalls that, on the eve of his first middle school game, because Steph had purposely ignored to wash the dishes, his mother disallowed him from playing. Despite the fact that Dell and Sonya were successful athletes, sports were not the household's first priority. The Curry siblings were aware of the order of priorities: faith come first, second came family, followed by academics before everything else, even sports.

When Dell was a child, the environment was not very friendly or conducive for an only boy growing up in a house full of girls, and a neighborhood rich in roaming bears. In the early seventies, before the end of the school year in Grottoes, Virginia, Jack Curry, Dell's dad, needed to find a quick solution that would keep Steph away from the woods and the roaming bears; he wanted to find a way for his son, Dell, to occupy himself in the summer, other than dolls or deadly animals.

Ultimately, using a tired utility pole, some fabricated steel brackets, and a fiberglass backboard, Jack Curry managed to fashion a rudimentary backboard and hoop, and in the process, managed to write basketball history by producing the ideal point guard, Stephen Curry, his grandson.

Jack's hoop was not in any way striking. Its best feature was the old street lamp that dutifully blinked over the court, spreading out its warm yellow light. However, this was part of Jack's plan all along because he understood that only those who truly loved the game and were aware of the commitment it took would hang around past dusk on this country court.

The backboard's soft wings were more forgiving than a gated fence, and the thick steel rim was not very accommodating because only shots perfectly directed at the center of the cylinder sailed through. The green metal breaker box right behind the hoop produced a constant hum that stole a shooter's concentration from the target. The wooden utility pole, on the other hand, was not squared to any landmark, and every shot made required instant, skilled recalibration.

Several years of toiling in the mud and sun honed Dell's smooth, lethal jumper, a shot that led him to a national title, a Virginia Tech scholarship, and a sixteen-year NBA career that ended in 2002. When Dell and Sonya finally gave birth to their first son, Wardell Stephen Curry II, he inherited more than just his Grandpa's name. He also inherited the hoop, as well as the deep enduring love for the game associated with it.

During his childhood, when they made frequent trips to Grottoes, Stephen and Seth, his younger brother, could hardly wait for the car to stop before they jumped out and raced to the back to shoot. Juanita, their grandma, whom everyone fondly refers to as Duckie, was aware that if she wanted a hello hug from her grand kids, she had to place herself between the hoop and the car. (Jack had passed away when Curry was two).

It is here that Stephen became obsessed with the long ball, as he strived to become the first member of the family to score from sixty feet. As he recalls, he always felt as though the lessons and love of the hoop had simply passed down to him.

He honed his ball handling skills dribbling through the tire tracks and rocks placed near the hoop, while the unforgiving rim and the unpredictable backboard, constantly tested his touch, subsequently inspiring the perfect, ridiculously high parabolic curve of his shot. The court also polished his composure, and ultimately, he acquired the Tao of Point Guard.

He admits that this place, inclusive of its rudimentary hoop, was visionary for him and irrespective of how rugged the court and hoop were, he had to make it work. According to him, the best way to be a great basketball player is to get creative, learn to adjust, be willing to try a different shot, a different move, a different lane, or a different angle, improvise, and make it work; there was no better place to nurture this type of creativity than on his grandpa's court.

In any case, it is hard for the Grizzlies fans to rattle you once you have consecutively hit one hundred free throws with real underfed bears literally lurking behind the tree line. Steph refers to his dad as Pops, and it is from his Pop's stories that he came to understand the constant solitary effort needed in a perfecting your game.

His most memorable tale was how each summer morning, after Dell's parents left for work, his sisters would take him to the back steps, press a basketball against his chest, and lock him out of the house. If he behaved well, that is, if he did not interfere, for his lunch, they would pass him a fried egg sandwich from the window.

About thirty minutes before their parents got back from work, the girls would unlock the door, dust Dell off, wipe his face, change his shirt, and swear him to silence. What did Dell then do with 8 hours of his day? Dell had nothing else to do but to perfect his jump shots, which later become the smoothest, effective, and efficient shots in the history of NBA; Stephen later mimicked this exact form.

Working on the seemingly ever-muddy court, Curry learned that the only sure way to keep the ball clean, safe, and in the same side was to make every shot. Stephen admitted that this link to perfection came from his grandpa and his hoop. You had to make the basket, or chase the ball out there, which was very terrible. There was no room for a miss. As Curry later stated, "As a shooter, this instills a certain quality in you without even knowing it."

When Jack passed away in 1991, at 58 from a sudden heart attack, he was just settling in to watch his son play the Lakers on television. When Dell got back to Virginia, he found the house flush with mourners then he went straight to his mom and gave her a light peck on the cheek, before weaving through the crowd and shutting himself in his room, devastated.

After some time, the family heard the dim, familiar noise coming from the hoop. Dell did not fully realize the effect of the basketball butterfly impact of Jack's hoop until he knew that he would have to pass over the same, exact lessons he had learned to Steph.

When Stephen Curry joined sophomore year at Charlotte Christian School, he was a skinny, 5 foot, 8, 150-pound teenager. His flip shot was weak and inefficient, and simple to block. It was then that Dell realized that for Curry to advance to the next level, he would have to scrape everything, and start building his shooting techniques from scratch.

The first few months were tense and frustrating for everyone in the family. Steph, who loves the game so much that he usually shoots 1,000 baskets before practice, admits that this was the only time that he truly hated shooting. Their court in South Charlotte is slightly different from the Grottoes one.

On the South Charlotte court, perfectly smooth concrete between the perfectly green lawns smear almost half of the court, and the court has professionally fitted top grade glass backboard, and a stucco-lined 2-car garage. Manicured crepe myrtles, that keep the ball from jumping into the sparkly pool, shade the court. However, Steph still endured an almost identical summer-long grind as his father endured, except for the fried egg sandwiches. Jackie fondly referred to this as the summer of tears. They survived through it, and Curry perfected his trademark smooth, low lift, lightning fast form, as well as a graceful overhead follow through.

Almost as soon as Stephen created the greatest shot in the game, he knew that it was not going to be sufficient. Even though he only had one-year experience as a point guard, which he had played during his last season at little known Davidson College, the Warriors picked him as the 7th overall pick in 2009, and then began rebuilding around him. After 3 years, chronic ankle complications brought doubt to his durability, ball handling, and defense, limiting him to 23 starts only in 2011-12.

Sonya, Steph's mum explains that his relatives played a significant role in raising him. Curry adds that he and his siblings considered it a blessing to grow up with such great influences in their lives. He recalls that, even though he numerously watched his father's games as a child, he still considers the ones between him and Seth, his little brother, to be the best of his childhood.

# Section 2: Steph's High School Years

For his high school education, Wardell Stephen "Steph" Curry II went to Charlotte Christian School in Charlotte, North Carolina, where he quickly started showing his prowess as a premier & professional quality basketball player.

His record at Charlotte Christian School is impressive. He and his brother, Seth, played together for two years there, where he received several awards including the team MVP (or Most Valuable Player), the all-conference, and all-state award when he sailed his team to 3 conference titles, in addition to 3 playoff appearances.

As tremendously surprising as it may sound, especially considering his tremendous achievement in high school basketball, Steph failed to land a single scholarship from a renowned conference school, which he very rightfully deserved, given the fact that he had attained a 48 percent shooting percentage from the other side of the arc.

Part of the reason for this is because most coaches and scouts from the big programs considered him"too short, too skinny", to make a name for himself in college basketball, remarks prompted by the fact that, at that time, Curry weighed 180 pounds, and was 6 feet tall.

When Dell's career in Toronto was nearing its end, Steph was an almost shockingly small and elfin-looking lad; he was only fourteen, just a kid. Still, he wanted to practice more and become a professional if he ever got the chance. That year, he led Queensway Christian's middle school team to an undefeated season, contributing 40 to 50 points per game.

If you take a closer glance at the team photo, Steph is maybe the 3rd smallest player, if you include his little brother in the roster. He had a long way to go to become a sure thing. He had a passion for the craft, and the subtle skill of a man born into the trade. However, he was no Peyton Manning (6ft 5). On the contrary, he was undersized, not strikingly athletic, and not blindingly quick.

Since he was relatively weak, Stephen would release his shot from the navel. Dell realized that this was inefficient because it was too methodical and easy to block. He decided to adjust his son's shot, forcing him to bring the ball over his head before letting go.

It took a considerable amount of time before Steph could master this shot. He recalled that, for 3 weeks, he had a hard time shooting outside the paint. He was terrible at it before he finally figured it out. He was a three-star recruit player, who did not appear in the list of national top 100 to 150 recruits made by such sports websites as Rivals and ESPN.

One scout actually gave him a score of 36 over 100 from his personal perspective. Nonetheless, Stephen Curry made it into mid major Davidson College, turning down offers from High Point, Virginia Commonwealth, and Winthrop. In reality, largely due to his Pop's Hall of Fame status in the college, his dream was to go to Virginia Tech, but he failed to land a scholarship there. In fact, the Hokies only extended him an invitation as a walk on. Instead, which as he state "because they had a good education system and a tightly knit community", he went for Davidson.

# Section 3: The College Years

Once Steph enrolled at Davidson College, he played for the school's basketball team for 3 years. During this time, he made such a significant impact on the Wildcats that he propelled them to several great performances. To the surprise of everyone who thought he was 'too skinny', he become the team's star player.

After high school, Steph picked up from where he had left off in high school, and continued to soar from there, significantly improving his game year after year. He kept improving his numbers, and made memories worth remembering for a long time.

In his first year at Davidson College, Curry made an instant impact, laying his foundation for future success. Prior to his first appearance, his head coach could hardly wait to see Steph Curry in action, famously exclaiming that he, Steph, was something special.

He did not disappoint or fall short of his coach's glory; Steph Curry went on to average 21.5 points per game while sporting a 40% three-point percentage and 46% field goal percentage. In just his second appearance as an undergraduate, Curry gave a preview of the dominance that was to come in his near future with a 32-point game, coupled with nine rebounds and four assists.

Curry also shattered the school's previous record for most points scored by an undergraduate by scoring his 502nd point. He helped lead the Davidson Wildcats to a Southern Conference regular season title. Curry was second only to

Texas' Kevin Durant in undergraduate scorers.

By the time his undergraduate year lapsed, he had amassed 730 points, 366 of which were three-pointers. Curry's success in his undergraduate year did not end there; he was selected to represent USA in the FIBA Under-19 World Championship, where he excelled. He was selected as the Southern Conference Undergraduate of the Year, tournament MVP, and the all-tournament team along with many other prestigious awards.

Sophomore year for Stephen Curry was nothing more than another chance to impress. He was the star-performer in most of Davidson's matches and stepped up to face stronger teams such as North Carolina, North Carolina State, and Duke. Even though the Wildcats lost all of these games by close margins, Curry was the standout player, averaging 24.3 points in these three games along with some spectacular assists and unselfish plays.

One of Curry's most memorable games was when the Davidson Wildcats played against UNC-Greensboro. Coming out of halftime in a 20-point deficit, he went off, making 41 points, and ultimately defeated UNC-Greensboro. As he increased his points per game and led the Southern Division with 25.9 points, 4.6 rebounds, and 2.9 assists per game, Curry's numbers skyrocketed once again.

Having done well and being a great player did not hinder his progress. After leading the Wildcats to a 20-0 Southern Conference record and a 26-6 regular season record, Steph spearheaded the Davidson team into their first NCAA victory in almost 40 years. This game was against Gonzaga, and

Steph worked his second half magic to pull the team through; next came the match between Davidson and the favorites, Georgetown.

In this game, Steph showed tremendous resilience when he brought his team back into the lead after overcoming a 17-point deficit to shockingly defeat Georgetown by four points. He led the comeback effort with 30 spectacular points, 25 of which came in the second half.

Steph Curry was just getting started with the win over Georgetown. In the next round, he overcame the opposition's top defender, Michael Flowers, and went on to score 33 points to ensure an easy win over third-seeded Wisconsin. This paved the way to Davidson's first Elite 8 appearance since 1969.

In the NCAA regional finals, in an attempt to seal a win, Steph pulled all the stops, but unfortunately, Davidson fell against the Kansas Jayhawks in a low scoring thriller where the Wildcats lost by an agonizing two points on the 30th of March 2008. That season, Curry made 162 three-point shots, setting a new record, along with a massive 931 points in total. He also increased his statistics in all other areas of his game to become a well-rounded basketball player.

His commendable awards in his sophomore year included the Most Outstanding Player of the Midwest Region in the NCAA Division 1. This award was special to him since it was the first time since 1994 that a player from a team that had not made it to the Final 4 received the award. He also got a nomination in the Breakthrough Player of the Year category.

It is during his sophomore year that Stephen Curry cemented his name in the basketball history books with many significant milestones. With that, Curry still had not yet finished his career with the Wildcats of Davidson College.

Following his great success in 2008, he was prepared to take on the big leagues: the NBA. However, he announced that he would play one last season for Davidson prior to his run for a spot in the NBA. Curry II wasted no time in preparing for the NBA.

In a loss against Oklahoma, he scored 44-points, a career high. He kept up this high scoring streak and led the Wildcats to many victories. One of these was against Winthrop, in which he dished out another career-high of 13 assists. He matched his highest score in a game with NC State.

In his junior year season, Wardell had enormous success. He reached many incredible milestones in a very short period. He surpassed the 2000-point mark in just 83 games. Shortly after that, he became Davidson College's second leading scorer in history. He did not stop there; a 34-point game against Georgia Southern pushed him ahead of John Gerdy, making him the Wildcats' highest scorer ever.

Under Stephen Curry's leadership, Davidson lost only a mere two games and won eighteen in conference play. Despite their impressive conference record and the lobbying of their coach and even coaches of other programs, Davidson failed to get a slot in the NCAA Tournament.

In the Southern Conference tournament quarterfinals, Curry

scored 43 points, the third highest points ever scored in the tournament. After a bullish run, Davidson eventually lost in the semifinals. At the end of the season, Curry II became the leading scorer for the NCAA tournament; while Davidson managed to secure a slot in the 2009 NIT Tournament where they were the sixth seed but went on to lose in the second round to Saint Mary's Gaels.

Steph concluded his college career with his best numbers yet; sporting an average of 28.6 points per game. In his final game for Davidson, he scored 26 points, nine rebounds, and five assists.

He also was named as NCAA All-American first team player. Stephen Curry chose to leave Davidson after his junior year. In his 104 total games at Davidson, Curry finished with averages of 25.3 points, 4.5 rebounds, and 5.7 assists per game. His 2,635 total points and 414 total three-pointers are Davidson records. Leaving Davidson was smart move for him because he was already one of the best players in college basketball. He was all set to move on to the NBA.

In his college seasons, Curry had many highs and lows. There are instances he went scoreless in a game because the opposing team coach often assigned two defenders to be on him at all times. As a result, this left his teammates with wide-open shots, which ensured a win for the team despite having limited Steph, the team's star player.

IN THE END, WARDELL STEPH LEFT DAVIDSON AS ONE OF THE BEST, IF NOT THE BEST, PLAYER THE WILDCATS HAVE EVER SEEN. AFTER LEAVING DAVIDSON, HE JOINED THE NBA AS A FIRST ROUND, SEVENTH OVERALL PICK TO THE GOLDEN STATE

# WARRIORS.

# Section 4: The NBA Years: From Rookie, To All Star, To MVP, To NBA Championship

Wardell Steph made a sound decision when he decided to claim eligibility for the 2009 NBA Draft. At this time, he had peaked at college basketball, and probably gone down in history as the best player to play basketball at Davidson.

With numbers similar to what he had, and the experience accumulated from playing on the US U19 team, with whom, in 2007, Steph won a silver medal, his chances of being a Top-10 Draft pick were immensely high. In his junior year of college, he had managed to break some impressive records including the all-time scoring record for Davidson and the Southern Conference, school career records for free throws, three-pointers, 30-point games, 40-point games, and the single season NCAA record for three-point field goals.

Steph Curry had a storied college career. Everything looked good for a kid whose only goal when he first started playing basketball was to be taller than Tyrone Curtis aka Muggsy, his dad's teammate from his Charlotte days.

## Three Pointers

In his second year at Davidson, Steph broke the record for the most three pointers in a single season nationally. In just 3 seasons and with 414 three pointers, he is currently ranked sixth in the NCAA Division 1 history.

In the '2012-13' season, he broke the league's record for three pointers in a single season with 272 three pointers

In the 2014-15 season, Curry shot 44.3 percent from three point range, breaking his own record with 286 three pointers.

He also managed to shoot the fastest 1,000 three pointers with 369 games – the previous holder had to play 457 games to achieve the same.

He won the NBA 3 point shootout in 2015 as well.

### NBA 2009 Draft

In a draft class considered be one of the weakest since 2000, when Kenyon Martin was selected as the top pick, Steph was selected seventh overall by the Golden State Warriors. Nevertheless, the class had a handful of All-Star potential players such Blake Griffin, James Harden, Ricky Rubio, and of course Steph Curry.

Blake Griffin was the odds-on favorite to be the first overall pick in the whole draft and the Clippers did not hesitate. They took the best big man available as the first overall pick. Almost every team taking part in the lottery desperately needed a point guard or shooting guard on their squad.

Minnesota held the best position as they had two consecutive picks in the Top 5. The Grizzlies gambled and picked Hasheem Thabeet, which later became a pure Darko Milicic case. Oklahoma City needed a shooter that would transfer the Westbrook-Durant tandem into a trio, but they picked James Harden before Curry and Rubio. The Kings surprised everybody when they selected Tyreke Evans because they desperately needed a true point guard, an element that they had been missing since the Mike Bibby era in Sacramento.

Minnesota had the chance to create one of the most compelling potential PG/SG combinations in recent NBA history. They could pick Rubio and Curry with their two consecutive picks, but they opted against it. They went ahead with Rubio but instead of Curry, they chose Syracuse guard Jonny Flynn. One of the reasons the Timberwolves cited as their reason for not drafting Curry was because he refused to train with the team before the draft and stated that he would not be willing to play for a team that did not have a coach (Kevin McHale had a questionable status at the time).

If Minnesota had made the right decision then and in the next draft, they could have ended up with a starting five that included DeMarcus Cousins (they picked Wesley Johnson in 2010 instead), Kevin Love, Curry and Rubio. At this point in the draft, Mike D'Antoni was rubbing his hands with excitement because reports said that he was impressed with Curry's performance in the two pre-draft exhibition games against the Knicks.

At the time, New York had traded their starting guard Quentin Richardson to the Memphis Grizzlies and they lacked a prolific shooter after getting rid of Jamal Crawford and ending the Marbury drama at the beginning of the year. Keeping all of this in mind, Curry would have become an instant starter on the team and a possible leader for the confused squad. It was a good scenario, but the Golden State made a decision that nobody expected.

They added Curry to a roster filled with undersized shooting guards led by Jamal Crawford and Monta Ellis. On draft day, they traded Crawford to the Atlanta Hawks for Acie Law and Speedy Claxton. It was distinctly clear, even back then, that the Warriors were clearing up some needed space for their future star guard.

In an interview, years later, Steve Kerr, General Manager of the Phoenix Suns, stated that at one point, the Phoenix Suns and the Golden State Warriors were in talks of a trade that involved Amar'e Stoudemire and Steph Curry. Amar'e would have gone to Golden State and on draft night, they would have traded Steph.

Fortunately, for Golden State, the deal never reached NBA

front offices because at the time, Stoudemire had some health issues. Larry Riley, then general manager of the Golden State franchise at the end of June 2009, can thank God for Stoudemire's health issues, because had the trade gone through, Golden State would not be in the position they are in today.

### First Warriors Contract

The Golden State Warriors did not waste time once they drafted Steph Curry. They signed Curry to a four-year contract on July 8, 2009 in a deal estimated to be worth $13 million, which was slightly above the NBA Rookie pay scale for that season. It was one of the weakest rosters the Warriors had drafted in years, which later proved to be an excellent opportunity for Curry to display his skills. Curry did not disappoint and started his NBA campaign with great authority.

In his first appearance as a Warrior, in a one-point loss against Houston, he scored 14 points, dished out seven assists, and had four steals. Wardell spent much of the first two months of the season adjusting to the NBA schedule. Curry had a couple of flashes like his performance against the Denver Nuggets when he recorded 26 points, five rebounds, six assists and three steals in a tight loss in that period.

Shortly after this, Monta Ellis suffered an injury. This meant more freedom for Curry on the court. He embraced the role of a floor general in the absence of Ellis and had two terrific games between January 23 and February 10, 2010. In a 30-point win against the Clippers, he set his first career-high in points when he scored 32 against New Jersey and produced his first triple-double with 36 points, 13 assists and 10 rebounds (which included 7/11 three-point shooting).

Steph Curry was part of the 2009 All-Star event participating in the three-point shootout where he lost in the second round to Paul Pierce. He scored 14 points in the Rookie-Sophomore game to help his team win. Until the end of the season, with five or more 30-point, five-assist games, he became a part of an elite group of players that included LeBron James and Dwyane Wade.

During Don Nelson's record-breaking 1,333$^{rd}$win against the Minnesota Timberwolves, Curry scored 27 points, had 14 assists, 8 rebounds and 7 steals. Many NBA analysts regarded this game as the best rookie performance of that year.

After Blake Griffin failed to play in the 2009-10 NBA season due to injuries, Steph Curry became a fan favorite for the Rookie of the Year (ROY) award. His only competitor was Tyreke Evans; mainly because of his ridiculous stats, (Tyreke became one of only three other NBA players in history that averaged at least 20 points, five rebounds, and five assists), it was tough competing against such a start line.

Curry on the other hand, finished the season with 17.5 points, 6 assists, 4.5 rebounds, and 2 steals per game. This was enough to finish second in the ROY voting and to be a part of the All-Rookie First Team. He led all first year players in assists, steals, and three-pointers made.

Curry's performance in his rookie season did not go

unnoticed in NBA circles. Shortly after the end of the '2009-10' NBA regular season, he received a selection to the US National basketball team. This came as a great comfort after the Warriors failed to qualify for the playoffs, and he failed to win the Rookie of the Year award.

Curry served as a backup guard for NBA All-Stars Kobe Bryant, Chauncey Billups, Russell Westbrook, and Derrick Rose. He averaged 4.6 points in nine games, with his best game coming against Tunisia where he scored 13 points on 62% shooting.

It is interesting to say that Coach Mike Krzyzewski was one of the first to reject Steph Curry in his search for a college scholarship. The Duke staff at that time had stated that the 18-year-old Charlotte Christian graduate was too skinny, too short and labeled him as a one-dimensional player. It was a noble thing for Coach K to admit, albeit later, his mistake and misevaluation of Steph Curry. After Team USA won the gold medal, Krzyzewski stated in an interview that Curry possesses a "cerebral game", not only being able to make shots, but also being able to make plays as well.

### Injury Problems

Steph Curry continued to improve leading well into his second NBA season. While he was on the World Cup campaign with the national team, it became more and more obvious that Golden State was trying to build around him. The first step towards this was surrounding Curry with better and big men to create a presence in the paint. David Lee was the first choice on the Warriors' wish list. The versatile power forward was acquired in a sign and trade deal that sent Anthony Randolph, Kelenna Azubuike and Ronny Turiaf to New York. Other notable signings included Dorell Wright and Lou Amundson.

Curry led the team in assists per game and managed to start in 74 games. He missed eight games due to an ankle injury, which was the first sign of upcoming problems in the next season. He had a solid season and played top-level basketball on a nightly basis with only a couple of bad games. However, he still lacked maturity; Monta Ellis, and his more experienced teammate, who led the team in scoring and minutes played, overshadowed him.

It became noticeable that if they wanted to make the playoffs anytime soon, the Warriors could not function with Monta and Steph on the same team. This observation would be the precursor to one of them being traded from the team later on.

Steph Curry is the definition of a competitor. Perhaps his favorite player to compete against in today's game of pro basketball is Oklahoma City's Russell Westbrook. Curry averaged 32 points, eight assists and two steals in three meetings against the Thunder in his second season.

He also beat Westbrook in the Taco Bell Skills Challenge during an All-Star Weekend hosted at the Staples Center in Los Angeles. Unfortunately, the Warriors yet again, failed to qualify for the playoffs.

Curry, however, ended the season with an average of 18.6 points, 3.9 rebounds, 5.8 assists, 1.5 steals and a 44.2% clip from three-point range. He also set a new single season

Warriors record for free throw percentage, previously held by Rick Barry from the 1977-78 season, after Curry hit 212/227 free throws (93.4%).

Aside from the Skills Challenge, he also won the NBA Sportsmanship award for ethical conduct on the court and his activities in the community. This meant a lot for Curry, a dedicated Christian who always tries to help fellow citizens in need.

At the end of the 2010-11 season, Steph Curry underwent surgery to repair torn ligaments in his right ankle, injuries received from multiple sprains during his first two seasons in the NBA. Meanwhile, the team tried to create a better roster that led by new coach and former NBA star point guard Mark Jackson. They also tried to sign DeAndre Jordan in free agency, but the Los Angeles Clippers matched their $43 million offer sheet to the then restricted free agent. The Warriors struck gold on draft day with the 11th pick when they selected Washington State University's Klay Thompson, a son of former Laker player Mychal Thompson. At the time of his signing, nobody could have predicted back then that Thompson and Curry would become perhaps the deadliest one-two combination in the NBA.

Nevertheless, the birth of this killer tandem would need to wait a little while longer because Steph only managed to appear in only 26 out of 66 games in the lockout-shortened season. He sprained his ankle multiple times during the season, first on January 4, 2012 and again on March 10 just after making his return from another mild foot sprain.

While Curry spent the entire 2011-12 season recovering from

ankle injuries and undergoing a season-ending surgery, newly appointed general manager Bob Myers remained active in the front office to continue sculpting the Warriors around Curry. His first move was to get rid of Monta Ellis and to make room for Curry's comeback next season while acquiring a strong big man. This showed the front office's faith in Curry even if he had been injury-prone the previous seasons.

Myers recognized the strong big man potential in, Andrew Bogut, a former number one pick from Australia. The trade that sent Bogut to the Warriors included three teams and saw Stephen Jackson off to the Spurs, Monta Ellis signing for the Bucks, and Richard Jefferson coming to the Warriors. This was only an interlude of what would follow in the next two seasons as the Warriors developed into a playoff contending franchise.

### Second Contract

After a disappointing 2011-12 NBA season, and yet another failed attempt by the Warriors to qualify for the playoffs, Steph Curry was fit for the upcoming season. The Golden State front office had made some key moves during the past year, and the newly reconstituted Warriors squad looked as good as the one that had eliminated the top seeded Dallas Mavericks back in 2007 in the first round of the playoffs.

Curry had the necessary help under the basket from two big men in David Lee and Andrew Bogut. He also paired up with Klay Thompson, who had a promising rookie campaign, in the backcourt. Harrison Barnes, a highly touted twenty-year-old athletic forward, also joined the team as a rookie and was expected to take over the starting role at small forward.

These player changes, and the inclusion of a couple of veterans such as Jarrett Jack and Carl Landry, sounded very promising. It was also the first chance for second year head coach Mark Jackson to mentor an injury-free Steph Curry.

During the summer break, Curry signed a new contract with the Warriors that kept him in the city until the '2016-17' season. The signing of the contract proved that the Warriors were serious and wanted to build their franchise around Curry.

The four-year deal worth $44 million, started to take effect in 2013-2014. Many analysts believe that the Warriors received a great bargain in signing their star player because other players such as Tiago Splitter, JaVale McGee, and DeAndre Jordan, who are on a contract similar to Curry's, make more.

In fact, Curry is not even the highest paid player on the roster (Iguodala, Lee and Bogut currently have higher annual salaries). Curry's history of ankle injuries and his willingness to accept an offer that would enable the Warriors to bring a big name free agent for next season are the main reasons why the contract was significantly below market value for a player of his caliber.

Curry looked like he had real focus at the start of the '2012-2013' season and there was great team chemistry under the guidance of Mark Jackson that immediately reflectedon Curry's game. In January, he averaged over 20 points in the first three months of the season and missed only five games due to ankle problems.

That February, he exploded with averages of 25.4 points and 6.9 assists. This included a monumental performance against the New York Knicks at Madison Square Garden when he netted a career-high 54 points with 11/13 shooting from behind the arc. The 11 three-pointers in the game brought him within second place on the all-time leading list, putting him behind Bryant and Donyell Marshall who had 12 three-pointers in a single game.

He also had a 47-point game against Kobe and the Lakers in April. This was not enough for Curry, who looked determined to break a more significant and more recent all-time record. Curry finally broke this at the end of the season when he broke Ray Allen's record of total three-pointers in one season, scoring 272 times from beyond the arc in 78 games.

By the end of the year, based on his outstanding season, Curry had made that 44-million dollars contract the "bargain of the century". Curry finished the 2012-2013 regular season averaging 22.9 points, four rebounds, 6.9 assists and 1.6 steals while managing to shoot with 45.3% accuracy from three-point land.

He won the Western Conference Player of the Month award for April and was praised by head coach Mark Jackson for being half of the most intimidating back court shooting duo in NBA history, also known as the "Splash Brothers" (with Klay Thompson as the other half of the duo). This was the season when Curry became an All-Star quality guard and led the Warriors to their first playoff appearance in his era.

The sixth seeded Warriors faced the Denver Nuggets in the

first round of the playoffs. Steph Curry single handedly eliminated the Nuggets in six games averaging 24.3 points, 9.3 assists, 4.3 rebounds, 2.2 steals while shooting 47% from the field. NBA media praised Curry as the Most Valuable Player of the playoffs because of his ridiculous stats and the fact that he had so much impact on his team while on the floor.

The Warriors faced the experienced San Antonio Spurs in the second round of the playoffs. Curry scored 44 points in the opening game in a heartbreaking double overtime loss. He averaged nearly 46 minutes per game in the first four meetings of the series, which took a big toll on his performance in game five when he scored only nine points and had four turnovers.

The Spurs went on to win the series 4-2 and reached the NBA Finals where they ultimately lost to the defending champions Miami Heat. Regardless of what happened in the Spurs series, Steph Curry proved he was the future of the Golden State Warriors, and with the help of his coach, Mark Jackson, he was capable of leading his team.

The trust of the franchise in Curry when they traded former star Ellis to build the team around him had been validated. It was also a sign for general manager, Bob Myers, to invest even more in the team and to bring another star player to complete the already intimidating starting five.

Bob Myers made the Golden State Warriors an even more formidable team when they signed veteran All-Star and versatile small forward Andre Iguodala as a free agent. Iguodala had a reputation for being one of the best passing wingmen in the game, and for being a very solid perimeter defender, something the team was in dire need of.

This signing created one of the best teams in the league, at least on paper, and improved the chances of playoff success for the Warriors in the 2013-2014 season. Steph Curry continued leading his team, finishing with averages of 24.0 points per game, 8.5 assists per game (both career highs), and 1.6 steals per game.

This has been his best season to date and the Warriors entered the playoffs again. They started from the sixth spot again and faced the Los Angeles Clippers in the first round of the playoffs. It was an interesting matchup between the two most successful players from the 2009 NBA draft class: Blake Griffin and Steph Curry. In a hardly fought and very controversial series, Griffin's Clippers managed to edge out Curry's Warriors in seven games. Both star players have had tremendous seasons and have become true leaders of their respective teams.

Curry managed to record his second triple-double of his career, to stay injury-free for the whole season, and to participate in the All-Star game after the fans voted him as their second choice in the West, behind Kevin Durant. Curry set another record in that season. He made 261 three-pointers which, coupled with his record-setting 272 the year before, gave him the record for the most three-pointers made in a span of two seasons with 533.

In addition, he and Klay Thompson set the record for most combined threes in a year with 484. These two really lived up to their nickname, the "Splash Brothers". Curry also made it to the All-NBA Second Team for the first time, further cementing his status as one of the top players in the league today.

### 2014 All-Star Game

Curry received a selection as a starter for the 2014 NBA All-Star game. It was his first appearance in his five-year career. Curry ended up placing second behind Kevin Durant in fan voting for the Western Conference starters. It was a great accomplishment for him, and a lot of buzz circulated a week before the game as everyone was talking about his sweet jump shot and three-point range.

Even Barack Obama, the then President of the United States, stated in an interview that Curry is the best shooter he has ever seen, including Chicago's South Side legends. Curry was the first All-Star starter for Golden State since Latrell Sprewell in the 1995 All-Star game and the first vote leader for a position since Rick Barry in 1976.

Curry started the All-Star game with 9 missed three-point shots out of 10 attempts. He only managed to score 12 points in the game. Noticing that he was cold from the floor, Curry instead focused on setting up his teammates. He dished 11 assists and helped Durant and Blake Griffin score 76 points combined, in the highest scoring All-Star game of all time. He also had one nice behind-the-back-through-the-legs dribble that sent LeBron James and James Harden chasing after his ghost.

After the game, Curry said that his bad shooting performance was partly due to long game breaks between timeouts and quarters. The East won the game after a three-year drought and fellow point guard Kyrie Irving received the Most Valuable Player title.

The All-Star game showed the world that Curry had developed into a more versatile player after his 2012-13 breakout season and his stats support that statement. He has set personal highs in points, assists, and free throw attempts per 36 minutes of play for the 2014 season. The assist rate, which measures possessions that ended with an assist from Curry, increased significantly to 41%.

However, the improvement in passing has not been the only win for the twenty-five-year-old product from Davidson. Curry has also improved his defense by limiting his foul rate and producing a defensive rating of 102. Curry's importance to the team manifests in the fact that when he was on the bench, Golden State was outscored by seven points.

### The Splash Brothers

Despite leading the Warriors to consecutive playoff appearances, management made the choice to fire Mark Jackson three days after their first-round exit at the hands of the Clippers. The players publicly voiced out their support for Jackson but ownership had seemingly made up their mind as reports of dysfunction in the team's coaching staff came out before their playoff run.

Because of 'philosophical differences' with Jackson, Brian Scalabrine, assistant coach, was reassigned to Santa Cruz, the team's D-League affiliate; two weeks later another assistant, Darren Erman, was fired because he secretly recorded conversations between coaches, staff, and players.

Jackson's firing, irrespective of the fact that he instigated the turnaround of the franchise, showed the fickle nature of the head-coaching job in the NBA. He was a master motivator, who immensely improved Golden State's once non-existent defense. However, many observers felt that Jackson's offensive sets were too stagnant and led to isolation plays most of the time.

He did not use Curry as an off the ball shooter and failed to utilize Andrew Bogut's fine passing skills from the post. The head honchos of the team were looking for a different direction and on May 14, 2014, they announced the hiring of TNT analyst Steve Kerr to a five-year contract reportedly worth $25 million.

Kerr won multiple titles with the Chicago Bulls and San Antonio Spurs as a player before serving as the President and General Manager of the Phoenix Suns from 2007-10.

Kerr also owns the NBA record for career three-point percentage with a clip of 45.5 percent. Curry was one of the most vocal supporters of Jackson, but the appointment of one of the best three-point shooters of all time, and an offensive-minded coach in Kerr could potentially lead to maximizing the potential of one of the league's most potent offenses, and even improve Curry's individual game as well.

In the off-season, the Warriors made some minor moves, including the signing of combo guards Shaun Livingston and Leandro Barbosa to be the relievers of the "Splash Brothers" to further strengthen the Warriors' already powerhouse backcourt.

The biggest move of the 2014 summer for the Golden State Warriors was not giving up Curry's Splash Brother Klay Thompson in exchange for Kevin Love. Before the Cleveland Cavaliers got Love via trade, the Golden State Warriors was one of the teams actively involved in the Kevin Love Sweepstakes. However, Love's former team, the Minnesota Timberwolves, was only interested in discussing the trade with the Warriors if the latter included Klay Thompson in their trade proposal.

Instead of getting the sharpshooting Love as their new power forward, the Warriors believed that keeping the Splash Brothers intact and making them the cornerstones of the team was the right way to move forward.

Golden State would then go on to re-sign Thompson to a four-year $70M contract extension. Although the temptation of getting a three-point shooting and rebounding demon in Kevin Love was a tricky situation, keeping Thompson was a no-brainer for the management.

If the Warriors had gotten Love, the entire offensive scheme would have changed with a new threat in the frontcourt. However, keeping Curry and Thompson together meant the continuity of the young core and the development of a backcourt that was emerging as one of NBA's best, especially after their participation in the gold-winning performance of Team USA in the 2014 FIBA Basketball World Cup in Spain.

The Splash Brothers' performance in the 2014 FIBA Basketball World Cup proved the value of both Curry and

Thompson as individual basketball players, and affirmed the Warriors' decision to keep the pair together. While Stephen Curry started all of Team USA's games, Klay Thompson's streaky shooting, and tough perimeter defense often led the mid-game spurts and little runs that broke games wide open for the Americans.

Although Cleveland Cavaliers guard Kyrie Irving received the tournament's MVP title in the 2014 FIBA Basketball World Cup, the contributions of both Curry and Thompson were invaluable in winning the gold medal. On the side of the players, the impact of playing for the flag went way beyond the statistics they produced.

Curry and Thompson returned to the Warriors more confident than ever and eager to prove themselves on the NBA stage too. After conquering the world stage, and winning the gold medal for their country, the next challenge for the splash brothers became winning the NBA title.

Steve Kerr's hiring as coach was the first move in that championship direction. As a former designated shooter for both the Chicago Bulls and San Antonio Spurs during some of their championship runs, Kerr had a grasp, on a first person level, of the value of shooters and the three-point shot to the game and to a successful title run.

Rightfully so, Kerr hit one big three-point shot after another for those two teams during his NBA career. With a coach who fully understood their game and value to the team, backing them, it was a mere matter of time before the Splash Brothers played beautiful music with their older Splash Brother in Coach, Steve Kerr. Early on during the regular season, Kerr's coaching philosophy seemed to work wonders for the team and Curry as Golden State got off to a scorching 8-2 start to lead the Pacific Division.

Two wins later and after defeating the Oklahoma City Thunder on November 23, the 10-2 Warriors were having the best start in franchise history. They did not stop winning. Stephen Curry averaged 27.5 points and four three-pointers per game in the next four games to finish the month of November on a high note. In addition, because all four were road games, the Warriors scored their first perfect road trip (5-0) since 1978 and only the second spotless away trip in franchise history.

Kerr had instilled variation such as running the offense through Australian center Andrew Bogut more than in previous years, allowing Bogut to create plays from the post, letting Klay Thompson facilitate the offense, and relieving Curry of the ball handling duties from time to time in the Warriors' offensive patterns. Kerr's system also brought the best out of Bogut as well as Thompson, who went on to show that he is also a very adept penetrator, not just a spot-up shooter, and a premier perimeter defender.

Still, it is not only in offense where they were good; the Warriors also showed tremendous improvement in their defensive efficiency, showing that Kerr placed an emphasis on the 'other' side of the game. More importantly, Curry began to flourish in Kerr's system by averaging 23.8 points, 4.9 rebounds, 7.9 assists & 3.26 three-pointers made per game and very efficient shooting percentages of 50.2% from the field and 92.8% from the free-throw line during the month of November.

The new system performed wonders for Curry's offense, allowing him to come off screens set by his teammates, and imitate some of the sets that the Atlanta Hawks use to free up their own sharpshooter Kyle Korver. Curry's game was not the only thing getting better by the day; his relationship with Steve Kerr also improved. Curry and his coach even engaged in shooting contests just to keep the Warriors' point guard sharp at all times.

This started with the highly publicized free-throw shooting contest between player and coach during the pre-season. In that much-documented video, Curry beat his coach by a single point. The friendly competition between player and coach did not end there; a couple more foul shooting contests and even a three-point contest that almost mimicked the one that Curry had with former Head Coach Mark Jackson in the previous season followed.

Slowly, Kerr gained Curry's trust and Curry trusted Kerr. With the relationship between star player and coach going very well, the Warriors started the season like a house on fire. As November ended, the 14-2 Warriors were the NBA's surprise leaders in a season where injuries altered the experts' predictions. The defending champions San Antonio Spurs, which had returned with their 2014 championship line-up intact, were the favorites to repeat and rule the Western Conference.

However, injuries to key players Kawhi Leonard, Tony Parker, and Manu Ginobili forced the Spurs to struggle after the first full month of the 2015 season. Along with the Spurs, the other 2014 Western Conference finalist Oklahoma City Thunder suffered a big blow when 2014 MVP Kevin Durant started the season on the sideline after suffering a Jones fracture and undergoing surgery during the offseason. During their first game of the 2015 regular season, Durant's sidekick, Russell Westbrook got his hand injured and he too was out of the Thunder line-up in November.

With these two title favorites hurting and the Los Angeles Clippers struggling to find their form, the fast start gave Curry and the Warriors more confidence to push further into the tough Western Conference. By December 10, 2014, the Warriors' winning streak had extended to 14 games, giving them the longest winning streak in franchise history.

This record extended to 16 before the Warriors lost to their eventual second round playoff opponents Memphis Grizzlies on December 16 in Memphis. On January 7, 2015, Curry became the fastest player in NBA history to make 1,000 career three-point baskets. He accomplished the feat in 369 games, which was 88 games faster than the previous record of 457 games set by former Orlando Magic three-point specialist Dennis Scott. Two weeks later, Curry and the Warriors established a new franchise record for consecutive home wins at 17. They added two more before losing to the Chicago Bulls on January 27, 2015. The loss to the Bulls would prove to be the team's final home loss of the regular season.

On January 23, 2015, Curry's Splash Brother, Klay Thompson, exploded for a career-high 52 points against the Sacramento Kings in a 126-101 blowout that gave the team a franchise best and league-leading 35-6 start. During that game, Thompson set the record for most points in a single quarter with 37 points during the third period of that game. He broke the previous record of 33 points shared by George Gervin, and Carmelo Anthony.

However, more important than Klay Thompson breaking that record and setting a career-high in points scored in a single game, Stephen Curry's unselfishness was the one thing that made that game more memorable. With Thompson scorching hot, Curry took just 11 shots in the entire game, 5.8 attempts fewer than his season average and scored just 10 points for the entire game.

Those 10 points scored would later turn out to be Curry's third lowest scoring game of the season, and it was not because he was struggling so much from the field, or that the opposition was defending him well. Rather, it was because he took a back seat and allowed Klay Thompson to grab the spotlight on the biggest night of his NBA career. Curry also finished the game with 11 assists, mostly to Thompson who went 13-13 from the field during the record-breaking third quarter.

Curry's basketball actions during that game proved that there was no sibling rivalry between the Splash Brothers because they genuinely liked each other as persons and players. Instead of competing for the limelight, they fed off each other and pushed each other to greater height. Moreover, because of this harmony, Curry and Thompson became the destructive offensive duo that propelled the Golden State Warriors to new heights in 2015.

Two weeks later, Curry proved that harmony and returned the favor on Thompson by putting up his best offensive output of the season, scoring 51 points in a 128-114 destruction of the Dallas Mavericks on February 4, 2015. Curry went berserk from the floor, hitting 16-26 shots from the field, including 10-16 from three-point distance as the Warriors erased a 42-25 first quarter deficit to win and improve their league-leading record to 39-8.

Curry poured in 26 points in the third quarter alone as the Dubs took the lead for good against the Mavericks. He looked unstoppable and hit three-pointers from as far as three to four feet behind the three-point line. Curry's 51-point effort gave the Splash Brothers yet another NBA record as their Golden State Warriors became just the seventh team in NBA history to have two different players score at least 50 points in a game in the same season.

At the end of the first month of the 2015 season, the 37-8 Warriors had a comfortable lead over their Western Conference rivals, and had become the team to beat in the West, just as the Atlanta Hawks were in the East.

Curry led the team in scoring in 19 of their total games and already had eight 30-plus points scoring nights by January 2015. He also led the Warriors in assists in all but five games up to that point. By January 31, 2015, Steph Curry had played in the entire Warriors' 45 regular season games, and was averaging 23.0 points, 8.1 assists, 4.7 rebounds, and 2.1 steals per game, which were better than his career averages. He was also making three three-pointers per game at a high 39.5% clip and was shooting a league best 91.5% from the foul line heading into the midway point of the season.

## The 2015 All-Star Weekend

As word of the Warriors' emergence spread, Stephen Curry's legend flourished. When the first the announcement for the set of fan votes for the 2015 NBA All-Star Games came in, Curry topped the list for the Western Conference with 549,095 votes. Out East, it was three-time top vote getter LeBron James leading the way with a league best 552,967 votes. However, while everyone expected James to be on top of the list, nobody expected that Steph Curry would surpass another former three-time leading vote getter Kobe Bryant of the Los Angeles Lakers in the Western Conference.

## Breaking Records

On March 24, 2015, the Warriors clinched the Pacific Division title for the first time since 1976 with a win over the Portland Trail Blazers. On that night, they also established the franchise record for most road wins in a single season with their 24th win away from the Oracle Center.

On March 28th, the Warriors set another franchise record for most wins in a single season with 60 wins. Win number 60 also assured the Warriors of home court advantage until the Western Conference finals. They would go on to break their franchise record for most wins seven more times and ended the season with the best record in the entire league at 67-15, becoming the 10th team in NBA history to win at least 67 games. In doing so, the Warriors claimed home court advantage for the entire 2015 post season as they hoped to replicate their regular season success in the playoffs, where they had not had much success in the past.

Before the Warriors' 2013 playoff appearance, they had missed the big dance for five straight years, including Curry's first three seasons in the NBA. In Curry's sixth seasons in the NBA, he had seen the playoffs only in the past three seasons and his first two cracks at the postseason both ended in first round defeats.

The 2015 season was different because the Warriors broke one franchise record after another. The Warriors had a first time coach in Steve Kerr and like the team he coached, he too broke the record for most wins by a coach in his first season in the NBA. Like his team and coach, Stephen Curry also broke several records during the 2015 season.

Aside from breaking his record for most three-pointers in a single season, Curry and Thompson also obliterated their own record for most three-pointers combined by two teammates with 525. The Splash Brothers set the former record of 484 last season.

Curry finished the season sixth in scoring (23.8 PPG), sixth in assists (7.7 APG), fourth in steals (2.04 SPG) and had a career best 4.3 rebounds per game in this season. His 44.3% conversion from the three-point area was also 4th in the NBA, while his 91.4% free-throw shooting percentage was the best in the league in this season. Curry also made a career-high 52 straight foul shots without a miss from March 9 to April 4, 2015.

With these record-shattering performances on both the team and individual players level, Stephen Curry erased all the criticisms previously pasted on his back: weak ankles, poor defense, and the inability to finish around the basket. Critics agreed that he was not the freight train that LeBron James, is and the complete greatness that Michael Jordan was, but he dominated the season in his own way: shooting threes as we have never seen before.

He changed the geography of pro basketball by putting a premium on the three-point shot more than any other player in its history. With all the accomplishments he made in this season, Curry was no longer the future of the NBA; his time had arrived.

### *The MVP*

With the Golden State Warriors emerging as the league leaders in the NBA team standings for the 2015 season, Stephen Curry's name began appearing in MVP discussions and deservedly so, since he was the motor that ran the best team on the league. However, Curry was not the only player having a standout season.

The New Orleans Pelicans' power forward Anthony Davis emerged as one of the top big men in the NBA with a breakout 2015 season. The first overall pick of the 2012 NBA draft was fourth in the NBA in scoring (24.4 PPG), eighth in rebounding (10.2 RPG), and number one in shot blocks (2.94 BPG).

Oklahoma City's ferocious floor general Russell Westbrook also had an incredible season wherein he recorded 11 triple doubles. Westbrook went on to became the first player since Michael Jordan who recorded 4 triple doubles in a row and in an impressive six over an eight-game span. Westbrook also became the seventh player in the league to have at least ten triple doubles in a single season since 1985-86.

However,with Kevin Durant injured, Westbrook's Thunder was struggling, as was Davis' Pelican's because of the injuries to starting PG Jrue Holiday, and sweet shooting forward Ryan Anderson. With their teams struggling, Westbrook's and Davis' MVP bid were both in jeopardy as 21 of the last 24 regular season MVPs came from teams with a Top 3 record and the fact that since 1982, the NBA's regular season MVP has come from a team with at least 50 wins.

That piece of historical data theoretically narrowed down the MVP conversation down to Stephen Curry and James Harden, who's Houston Rockets, was surging in the second half of the season even without All-Star center Dwight Howard, who, due to a knee injury, was out for a handful of games. Harden, who incidentally, played with Curry and Anthony Davis in the US Men's, 2014 FIBA Basketball World Cupbasketball team, was also having a career season of his own. Harden's 2015 season averages of 27.4 points, 5.7 rebounds, 7.0 assists, 1.9 steals and 0.7 blocks were all career highs. The player popularly known as "The Beard" had 10 40-point games and 33 30-point games in 81 regular season games played. He became the first player in the Houston Rockets' franchise history to have two 50-point games in a single season. He also led the Rockets to their first ever division title since 1994.

What made Harden's 2015 season impressive was the fact that he was able to accomplish all these without Dwight

Howard who, due to a knee injury, had 41 games in this season. On the other hand, Stephen Curry had a very talented team around him that helped him get the victories for Golden State. Nevertheless, Curry received the 2015 NBA MVP nomination shortly before the Warriors played Game 2 of their second round series against the Memphis Grizzlies.

Statistically, Curry was truly the Warriors' MVP. He was a plus 11.5 points for his team during his 80-game appearance in the regular season. Overall, the Warriors scored 920 more points than their opponents did when Curry was on the floor. Curry received a total of 100 out of 130 first place votes from a panel consisting of 129 sports writers and broadcasters, plus the 1 vote coming from a fan poll on NBA.com.

As expected, Harden came in second with 25 first place votes while four-time MVP LeBron James finished at third place with five first place votes. Rounding off the Top 5 were Westbrook and Davis. Curry became the Warriors' first MVP winner since Wilt Chamberlain in 1960, back when the Warriors were still playing for Philadelphia. He also became the second player in league history to win the MVP and play for a team with 65 wins. The only other player to achieve that feat was Earvin "Magic" Johnson in 1987 when Magic led the Lakers to the 1987 NBA title. Will lightning strike twice for Curry and the Warriors?

### 2015 Playoffs

After opening the season with a 20/1 odds to win the NBA title in the Las Vegas Super book, the top-seeded Golden State Warriors started the 2015 postseason as the top title favorites along with LeBron James and his Cleveland

Cavaliers. Steph Curry found himself playing against FIBA World Cup teammate and fellow MVP contender Anthony Davis in the first round of the playoffs. Davis willed his New Orleans Pelicans to the playoffs by edging out the Russell Westbrook-fueled Oklahoma City Thunder in the final day of the regular season. In contrast, the Warriors and Curry had already sealed home court advantage a couple of weeks earlier.

Their match-up looked like a classic battle between David and Goliath, only that the little Stephen Curry is the Goliath while the long and lanky Anthony Davis is the David. Curry led the Warriors to a 106-99 win over the Pelicans in Game 1 and although the final score was close, it did not show the fact that Steph Curry dominated the game despite shooting just 4-13 from three-point distance. Curry shot 13-25 from the field and scored a total of 34 points as his Warriors led 84-66 at the start of thefourth quarter.

Davis, on the other, scored 20 of his 35 points in the final period to lead a furious Pelicans' rally, but Curry and the Warriors held on to win the opener. The Pelicans opened Game 2 strong and held a 13-point lead in the first quarter before the Warriors exploded in the second period to take the lead for good.

The Dubs leaned on Klay Thompson's 26 points and Curry's 22 markers plus six dimes to beat the Pelicans 97-87 and take a 2-0 lead to Game 3 in New Orleans. If we thought that the Warriors' second quarter comeback in Game 2 was impressive, Steph Curry pulled a rabbit out of his magical hat in a Game 3 performance that was one for the ages.

Down by 20 to start the fourth quarter and behind by 17 points with six minutes left to play, Curry spearheaded one of the most spectacular comebacks in NBA playoff history, a comeback punctuated by a miraculous three-pointer at the buzzer that sent the game to overtime.

In the extra period, Curry hit the first basket of the overtime, another three-pointer, that gave the Warriors a lead they never relinquished in that character-defining 123-119 Game 3 win in New Orleans, Again, Curry struggled on the field, shooting just 10-29 of his shots which included a playoff record tying 18 three-point attempts (with just 8 connections). Nevertheless, he not only scored a game-high 40 points, but also hit one big basket after another and those clutch buckets finished the Pelicans, not just in Game 3, but also throughout the series. Still shocked after their Game 3 collapse, the Pelicans were swept in Game 4 with a score of 109-98. Curry led the Warriors once again with 39 points on 11-20 shooting from the field. He made 7-11 on uncontested shots as the Warriors advanced to Round 2 of the playoffs for only the third time since 1991. With Mike Conley sitting out Game 1 to recover from a surgery to repair broken facial bones, the Warriors picked up where they left off and shrugged off an eight-day inactivity to roll to a 101-86 series opener win behind Curry's 22 points and 7 assists.

Just as everyone thought Curry and the Warriors would steamroll past the Grizzlies, the team with the motto "Grit and Grind" did what only two other teams had done in the 2015 season: beat the Warriors at the Oracle Arena. The Warriors entered Game 2 with a 21-game home winning streak and a record of 42-2 at home.

However, the return of a masked Mike Conley inspired the Grizzlies. Conley hit his first four shots, and outdueled Curry to give Memphis a 97-90 win and deal the Warriors their first home loss since January 27, 2015. More importantly, the Grizzlies stole home court advantage and headed home for Game 3 oozing confidence.

In Game 3, with the Memphis' defense swarming him like a sleuth of hungry bears, Curry struggled. Collectively, the Warriors went 12-31 on open shots while Curry shot a mere 8-21 from the field, and 2-10 from three ball, one game after going 7-19 from the floor and 2-11 from three-point land.

For the first time in the 2015 season, the Warriors looked very vulnerable and Memphis appeared to prove the cliché 'offense wins games but defense wins titles'. Down 2-1 in the series, Curry recorded the ninth 30-plus scoring game of his playoff career in Game 4 with 33 points. Looking every bit like the MVP he was, Curry pumped in 21 points in the first half as the Warriors took a 17-point halftime lead and coasted to the finish. With the series tied at 2 games apiece, the Warriors retreated home to the Oracle Arena and demolished the Grizzlies 98-78 in their best game of the series. Curry scored 18 points on six three-pointers while adding seven boards and six steals in an all-around performance where he broke Ray Allen's record for the fewest number of postseason games to make 100 three-pointers. Curry accomplished the feat in 28 games, or 7 games less than Allen did. He also became the 10th player in the last 30 years to score at least 18 points in a playoff game exclusively from three-pointers, and the first player in NBA history to hit six three-pointers and have six steals in a playoff game.

Two nights later, in Game 6, when he hit a Hail Mary from beyond half court to end the third quarter, Curry delivered the dagger that ended Memphis' season. The Grizzlies were then making a run, cutting a 15-point second quarter deficit down to just one late in the third period. The Warriors were up five points when Curry snatched a loose ball in the closing seconds of the third quarter and threw the 62-foot bomb that swished the nets.

With the Grizzlies and their fans stunned, Curry punctured the nets with one three-pointer after another in a scorching finish that saw him set a Warriors' team record with eight three-pointers. Curry finished with 32 points, 10 assists, and 6 rebounds to send the Golden State Warriors to their first Conference Finals' appearance since 1976.

On May 18, 2015, the second seeded Houston Rockets completed a near improbable comeback from 3-1 down in their second round playoff series to stun the Los Angeles Clippers and advance to the Western Conference Finals.

# Section 5: Steph Curry's Impact on Basketball

Since he enrolled at Davidson College at the age of eighteen until now, Curry has influenced numerous lives, organizations, and associations, and immensely changed the game of basketball as a whole. The biggest reason for his success is his dedication: he is a highly dedicated individual who has clearly defined goals; throughout his professional career, and personal life, he has repeatedly proven his dedication to personal excellence.

Curry shook things up when he reached the NCAA Elite 8 in 2008, and his team relegated top teams including Georgetown, Gonzaga, and Wisconsin. This affected not only Davidson College, but also the whole college basketball world in general. Curry proved that even smaller Division 1 schools could build a great team, improve their organization in a span of a year, and produce one of the biggest prospects in the NBA draft talent pool. He also proved wrong all major NCAA programs that rejected him because of his size. His play made a big statement to the world.

Because of Curry, nowadays, college organizations, and NBA scouts give more and more credit to basketball IQ, shooting technique, floor commanding, and many other intangibles traits previously overlooked. It is easy to see that Curry has influenced how young prospects appear in the eyes of coaching staffs. As a result, in the near future, it will be difficult to attain a selection as the number one draft pick solely based on vertical jump, wingspan, strength, and other purely physical attributes.

What Steph Curry achieved in his three years with the Wildcats was incredible. He faced a huge test when initially entering the NBA, having to answer the question of whether or not he could transfer his talents to the NBA level. There were many skeptics among them basketball experts and general managers before the 2009 draft. The skepticism was probably why Curry ended up as the seventh pick for the Golden State Warriors behind players like Hasheem Thabeet and Jonny Flynn, who are now both out of the league.

Now in his fifth NBA season, Curry has transformed the Warriors squad from a perennially lottery-bound team, into legitimate title contender.

They have made the playoffs in consecutive seasons, a feat that has been accomplished only once in the past thirty-seven seasons of the franchise (1990-91 and 1991-1992 seasons-their famed "Run TMC" era when they had former all-stars Tim Hardaway, Mitch Richmond, Chris Mullin, and Don Nelson, the immensely accomplished coach).

Curry has managed to accomplish all this thanks to his impeccable work ethic and positive attitude towards life. His crazy workout sessions receive acclaim today. However, since his high school days, Curry is widely regarded for being a hard worker (in terms of practicing his game).

He was once an attendee of a Kobe Bryant camp. According to one coach, Curry would start training one hour before anybody else was out on the court. Before the actual practice began, he had already made over a hundred shots and would always try to make at least five free throws in a row after the practice finished. No matter how big or small the game, his family was there for him and taught him how to be a good person and achieve his goals through the help of Christianity.

All of this paved the way for Curry to become not only a great player and dedicated father, but also a respected member of the community. Curry goes out of his way to help in the community as much as he can; one proof of that is the story about his wedding gifts. Curry does not just show his unselfishness in NBA games, or by signing an undervalued contract worth $44 million, but throughout his life as a whole.

On October 1, 2013, Curry signed a five-year shoe contract deal with fledgling apparel brand Under Armour, making him their main endorser. This was a big step for him because he wore Nikes all of his life, and represented the brand in his first four years in the NBA. This speaks volumes about Curry's marketability that a brand on the rise like Under Armour wanted him to be their top ambassador.

Under Armour has on their roster, guards like Brandon Jennings of the Detroit Pistons, Kemba Walker of the Charlotte Hornets, and Greivis Vazquez of the Toronto Raptors. Curry explained that the biggest factor he considered when deciding to switch shoes was that he was very comfortable during his meeting with Under Armour representatives and with them having fewer athletes to cater to, more people can be assigned to work with him in customizing his shoes which are very important to him due to his ankle injury history. Another deciding factor he cited was the way the brand intended to market him, as an underdog. As he put it via an interview with Complex

Sneakers, "Under Armour always talks about that underdog mindset that follows them in the basketball world, and that's how I've been my whole career."

Last October, through its CEO, Kevin Plank, Under Armour announced that in 2015, Curry would be getting his first signature shoe. According to reports, the shoe will bear the name UA Curry 1. The brand made a run at prying Kevin Durant away from Nike, with an audacious 10-year $285 million offer, but Nike exercised their right to match it and as a result, Durant stayed put.

Curry has substantially influenced his community's everyday life. He has changed how drafters perceive prospects, taken the name of his beloved Davidson College to the highest possible level, and completely transformed a dying Warriors franchise. Steph Curry has created a public image of a true role model for young NBA fans. The truly amazing thing is that he managed to do all of this at the young age of twenty-five while remaining a dedicated family man and a true member of a local Christian community.

# Stephen Curry's BEEF Basketball Routine

Here is a breakdown of Steph Curry's shooting foundation named B-E-E-F and taught to him well as a kid. This is easily practicable by anyone: child, teenager, or adult.

### The BEEF Simple Training Routine

BEEF is an acronym standing for:

### Balance

With your feet shoulder width apart, place your dominant foot slightly in front of the other foot, about 6 inches, and bend the knees for proper foundation.

### Eyes

Maintain focus on the rim's front. Three hooks, that are always facing your direction, and are approximately as wide as a basketball hold up the net; lock your eyes on this target, and try putting the ball over the hooks. Rather than shooting for the back, hold up the net.

### Elbow

Bend your elbows and keep your upper arm parallel to the ground and vertical to the basket so that it is stacked, instead of hanging out loosely like chicken wings.

### Follow Through

It is necessary to follow through with all the shots. This will help you achieve a better arch while shooting, as well as provide better ball rotation.

# Section 6: Legacy and Future

Stephen Curry transformed Davidson College. McKillop, Davidson Wildcats coach said that it is rare to find a player that not only leaves an imprint on a program, but who also puts all his energy into developing his team's spirit. Curry returned the compliment by saying that coach McKillop helped him achieve his goals by explaining his (McKillop's) vision for Curry's career and that being of similar faith, his coach always kept him grounded. He added that McKillop was a great leader. Curry's three seasons at Davidson will be remembered for many generations to come. He is one of six players in Davidson history that made it to the NBA and the first after Brandon Williams, who played for the Warriors in the 1997-98 NBA season.

His basketball exploits is not the only reason why Curry is still beloved at Davidson. Many teammates, schoolmates, and team staff members gush about his positive attitude and friendliness towards everyone. They all claim that his fame has not changed who he is as a person, that he is still very humble and approachable as he was in college.

Lauren Biggers, a college friend, said that most Davidson alumni want to identify with him; as Biggers put it:

"Stephen is kind of a way for the rest of the world to learn that", she a I think alumni are really attached to him in that way. Now you can s you know Stephen Curry? That's my guy, that's my school." "I went Carolina, but I would never be like 'Yeah, Michael Jordan is my guy."

Even though he inherited NBA genes, Steph Curry did not

enter college basketball as a top prospect. He developed into a scoring machine at Davidson and as much as he received from the school, he gave back in equal measure.

After rejection from a couple of NCAA division teams including Duke, Curry decided to join Davidson. It is interesting that just a couple of years later, after his second year in the NBA, Curry received selection for the United States national team led by Duke's Coach K. Curry developed a close bond with coach McKillop and his teammates at Davidson. He averaged 25.3 points for the team in three years and led the team to the Elite 8 tournament in 2008.

In that year, the Wildcats maintained a 20-0 Division record and earned the 10th seed for the NCAA tournament. In the first game, played against Gonzaga, the team was losing by as many as eleven points at the start of the second half, but Curry put on a heroic display, managing to score thirty points in the second half. This gave the Wildcats their first win in an NCAA tournament since 1969.

Something similar happened in the second round as well. While Curry only managed five points in the first half against Georgetown as his team was trailing by up to seventeen points at some point, Curry managed to score up to 25 points in the second half thus helping his team to advance to the next round. Georgetown was the second seeded team in the nation that year.

The entire nation took notice of Curry's talent when the Wildcats ended up losing to the top seeded Kansas Jayhawks right after winning another battle against third seeded Wisconsin. Curry actually managed to break multiple records during this process. For instance, he broke the record of the most three-pointers in a season and joined an elite group of players to score more than 30 points in their first four games of an NCAA tournament. With his performances over a period of three years, Stephen Curry made sure the Davidson's name remains engrained in basketball fans minds.

Now he has transferred his work ethic, attitude towards the game, and personal values into his NBA career. He has stated in an interview that he felt that God wanted to use him in the league to show that not all successful athletes live the celebrity lifestyle that comes with all the money and fame. To his wife Ayesha, he is a very dedicated and loving husband; to his daughter Riley, he is a loving father.

The future looks bright for Steph Curry, whom at the age of 25, has already left a significant legacy at Davidson College, and in the NBA. Wardell Steph Curry, the record holder for total three-pointers made in a regular season in the NBA and in the NCAA has a very optimistic future ahead of him.

Steph Curry is emerging as one of the greatest point guards of the modern era. Some pundits have even pronounced him as the best shooter of all time, ranking him above shooting legends Ray Allen (who holds the NBA record for three-point shots made) and Reggie Miller (whom Allen surpassed). They claim that this is because of the degree of difficulty of his shots. Most of the time, because he is the team's primary ball handler, Curry has to create his own shot through a maze of dribble moves such as the crossover and hesitation dribble as opposed to just catching it in rhythm and shooting as most shooters have the luxury of. LeBron even gave him a compliment that he made Mario Chalmers dizzy when Curry gave him three "hesis" (hesitation dribbles) before shooting over him.

Steph is also the active leader in career three-point percentage with a 44.0 percent clip, and is second all-time to his current coach, Steve Kerr. It will be exciting to see years from now how he will go down in the record books. In addition, Curry has also proven that he is more than just a deadly shooter and scorer. In the eyes of many coaches and fellow players, he is one of the most complete point guards in the league.

In Mark Jackson's system, he showed that he is very open to facilitating for his team while scoring in bunches, and now in new coach Kerr's system, he is effective off the ball as he is on the ball. This aside, his shooting which made him famous, is a testament to his versatility and his willingness to expand his game.

Most basketball junkies eagerly select Curry as one of the top 3 picks in fantasy drafts because of the well-roundedness of his stat line. Curry's underdog story has also led to comparisons between him and another "famous" small player, Allen Iverson. The similarities probably end in their stature and scoring ability as both have had very different paths to their careers. Curry grew up in a loving family, with loving parents by his side while the mercurial "AI" had a very difficult upbringing with a single mother and a non-existent father.

# Conclusion

When asked about Steph's future, Curry's college coach, McKillop summarizes it best:

"Steph has a future in whatever endeavor he decides to pursue. If Steph wanted to run for the mayor of Charlotte, or the governor of the state, if Steph wanted to be a coach, if Steph wanted to be an entrepreuneur, Steph Curry will accomplish it."

How about going down as one of the greatest shooters in the history of the game? Well, only time will tell...

Thank you again for reading this book!

I hope this book was able to help you to learn more about Stephen Curry. The next step is to research more about him as well as watch him play just to see why he is the greatest shooter of our time.

Finally, if you enjoyed this book, would you be kind enough to leave a review for this book on Amazon?

Thank you and good luck!